A Doubleday Activity Book

LEARNING TO READ

IS FUN

Illustrated by Marjorie Thompson

DOUBLEDAY & COMPANY, INC.

Garden City, New York

ISBN: 0-385-03933-6
LIBRARY OF CONGRESS CATALOG NO. 63-17341

PRINTED IN THE UNITED STATES OF AMERICA
9 8 7 6

CONTENTS

Note to Teachers and Parents

It is assumed that your child already knows how to read a number of very simple words, and has mastered a reading vocabulary covering the 200 or so basic words of the language. It is taken for granted that words like ME, SEE, TO, IT, COW, will be recognized by him.

This book, then, is for the child who desires to progress somewhat beyond the rudimentary reading knowledge one ascribes to children of 6 and 7—to children who know the alphabet and can recognize the most common and simplest short words.

The reading method employed in this book is a simple one. In each lesson, the child is presented with a list of rhyming words. To enliven the words and give them greater meaning, very simple definitions are given. Each definition is to be read by the parent or the teacher to the child.

After he has gone over a word list several times, the child is shown a list of these same words—but in each word, some letters are missing. The child is asked to fill in the missing letters, using picture clues to help him identify the word. This exercise looks like—and is—a challenging puzzle. The child will readily respond to this pleasant learning game.

A story then follows, the story employing the words the child has just learned. He should soon be able to read the story by himself.

The stories in this book are exceptional — imaginative, light-hearted, full of the child's own sense of humor and fun. These are stories he will really enjoy, not senseless repetitions of meaningless phrases. To be able to read truly entertaining stories all by himself is the reward for effort expended in working on his lessons. It is, in fact, the reward he will derive for the rest of his life out of the pleasurable experience of reading.

Working with this book should be fun, both for you and for your child. The lessons will be gratifying and pleasurable if you observe a few rules:

1. As soon as your child shows signs of fatigue or disinterest, stop the lesson. One lesson a day is usually enough. If your child is exceptionally eager, perhaps two lessons may not be excessive, but not more. Always try to terminate the lesson *before* your child becomes tired.

2. As you progress through this book, be sure to review the lessons you have already done. There should be some review every day. Going back several pages will not bore your child; on the contrary, if he now reads some former lessons with ease, he will get a sense of accomplishment which will serve to increase his confidence in tackling new words and new lessons.

Learning to read is largely a matter of visual memory. The more the child sees any particular word, the more likely he is to fix that word in his mind and to remember it. Bear in mind that words that are quite familiar to you are brand new to the child. Seeing them once or twice—or even fifteen times—is not always sufficient to imprint them in memory. Memory feeds on constant repetition and association—on day-in-and-day-out review.

When your child has completed this book, he will not find it difficult to learn new words. Of course, reading one book will not turn him into an accomplished reader. But, if he has thoroughly mastered LEARNING TO READ IS FUN, he will have acquired a solid foundation on which he can readily build a more extensive vocabulary.

Here's to many pleasant hours!

The Publishers

OO WORDS

Here are some words which contain the letters oo.

MOO	*Cow talk.*
COO	*Pigeon talk.*
BOO	*Ghost talk.*
ZOO	*A place where wild animals live.*
TOO	*Also.*

Fill in the right letter on each line.

____ oo

"I WANT ONE, ---."

____ oo

____ oo

____ oo

____ oo

O O SOUND

Here are words which sound like the OO words, but some are spelled differently.

SHOE	*What you wear on your foot.*
SUE	*A girl's name.*
DO	*To make something.*
YOU	*Yourself.*
THROUGH	*You go through a gate.*
BLUE	*The color of the sky.*
WHO	*Which person?*
COO	*The sound that doves make.*

Fill in the missing letters.

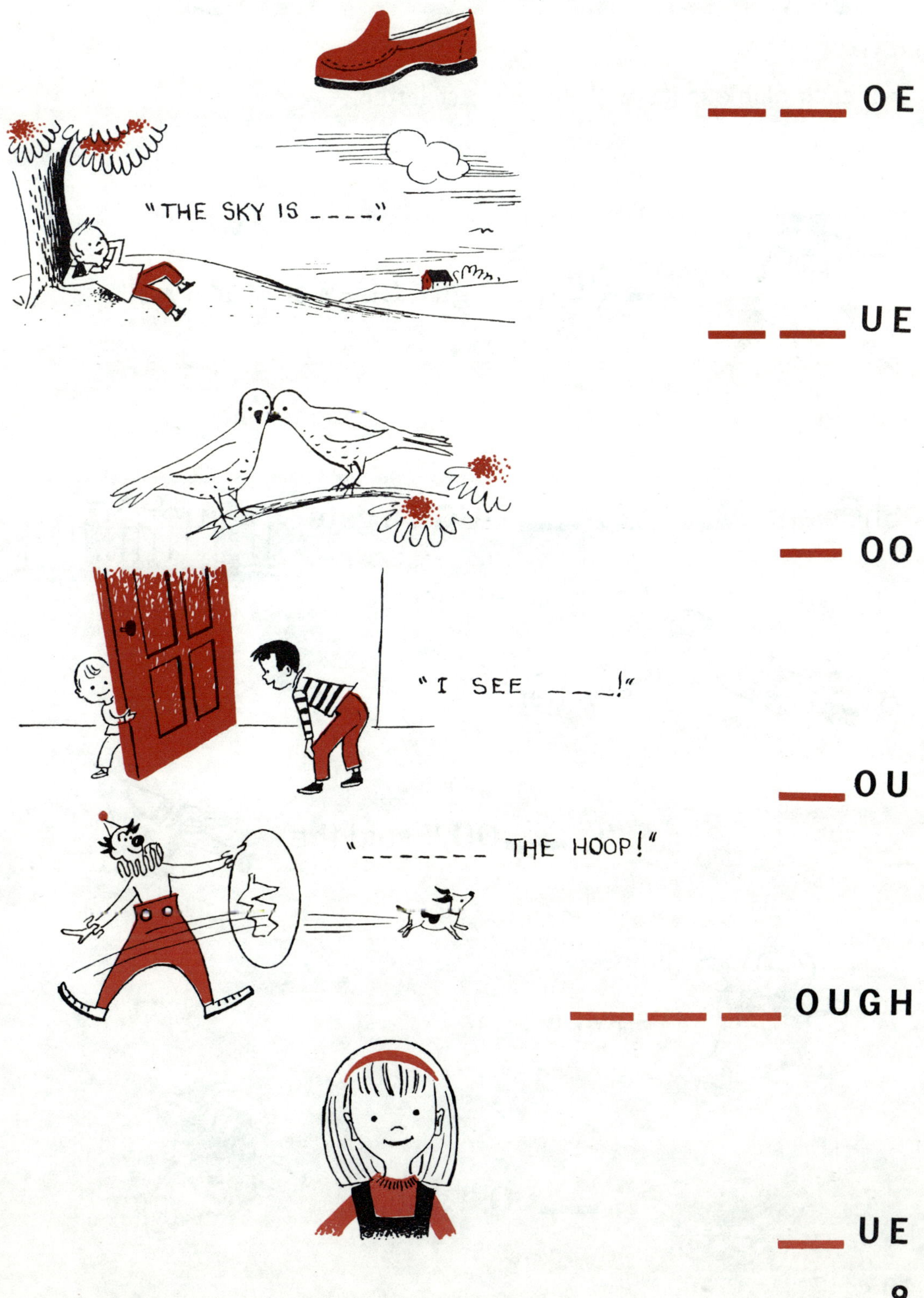

THE BAD COW

Fill each blank space with the correct letter.

__UE was a girl. She went for a walk.

She went __ __ __ OUGH a gate.

A  saw her.

"__OO," said the 

A  saw her.

"__OO," said the 

Then what do you think that  did?

She sat on ___ UE'S  ___ ___ OE.

 ___ UE told that 

" ___ OU should be in the ___ OO!"

Do you think so, ___ OO?

ED

Here are some words which contain the letters ED.

RED	*The color of a cherry.*
BED	*What you sleep in.*
FED	*To have given food.*
SLED	*What you slide on when there is snow.*
LED	*To have made someone follow you.*
SPED	*To have run fast.*
FLED	*To have run when you were afraid.*
WED	*To marry.*

Fill in the missing letters.

__ __ED

__ED

__ED

__ED

__ED

__ __ED

EAD

Here are some words which sound like the ED words, but are spelled EAD.

BREAD	*The outside parts of a sandwich.*
THREAD	*What Mother uses to sew with. Thread comes on spools.*
HEAD	*The top part of you, from hair to chin.*
INSTEAD	*In place of. "Let's eat cake instead of pie."*
AHEAD	*To be in front of.*
SPREAD	*To lay out. You spread a tablecloth.*
DEAD	*Not alive.*

Fill in the missing letters.

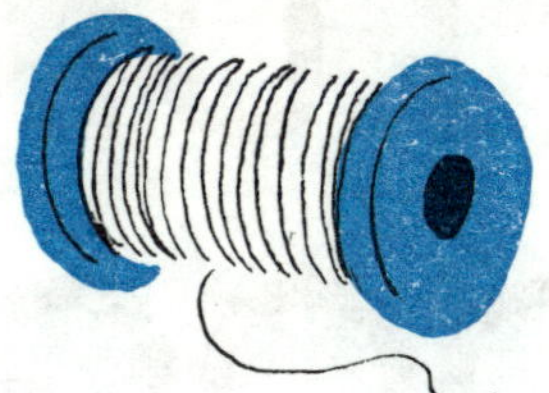

___ ___ ___EAD

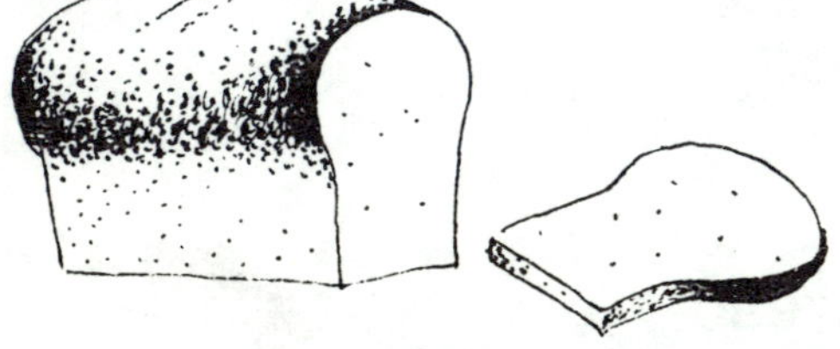

___ ___EAD

"STAY NEXT TO ME.

DON'T RUN _ _ _ _ _!"

___ ___EAD

"I MUST _ _ _ _ _ _

THIS TABLECLOTH."

___ ___ ___EAD

___EAD

"_ _ _ _ _ _ _ OF CAKE,

LET'S BUY A PIE."

___ ___ ___ ___EAD

THE FUNNY DOG

Sue had a dog. She fed the dog bread.
But he wanted thread, instead—red thread.

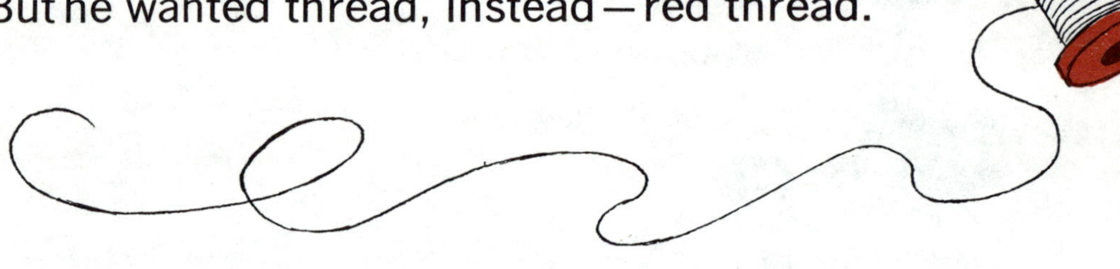

The dog took a ride on a sled. Did he do it for bread?

No, he wanted just thread—red thread, at that.

What could Sue do?
She gave him red thread.

Sue gave the dog a ball, a little ball.

But he wanted a shoe, instead
—a blue shoe.

The dog stood on his head.
For a ball?
Not at all.

For a shoe— and it had to be blue.

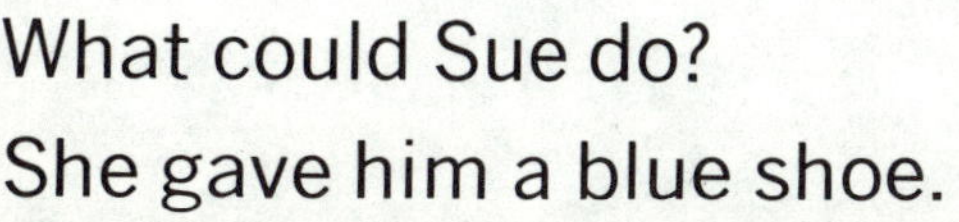

What could Sue do?
She gave him a blue shoe.
Then she led him to bed, with the shoe and the thread.

EEL

Here are some words which have the letters EEL.

HEEL	*The back part of your foot.*
EEL	*A snake-like animal.*
PEEL	*To take off the outside. You peel an orange.*
KNEEL	*To rest on the knees.*
WHEEL	*A wheel turns around. Cars have wheels.*
FEEL	*To touch.*
STEEL	*A very hard metal, used in building skyscrapers and bridges.*

Fill in the missing letters.

__ __ EEL

__ EEL

__ EEL

__ __ EEL

__ EEL

__ __ EEL

EEL SOUND

Here are some words which sound like EEL words, but are spelled EAL.

MEAL *Dinner is a meal.*

VEAL *The meat of a calf.*

SEAL *A dark, shiny animal which swims well.*

STEAL *To take something which does not belong to you.*

REAL *Not make-believe; not false.*

HEAL *To cure.*

EEL or EAL

DO YOU KNOW WHICH?

Fill in the missing letters.

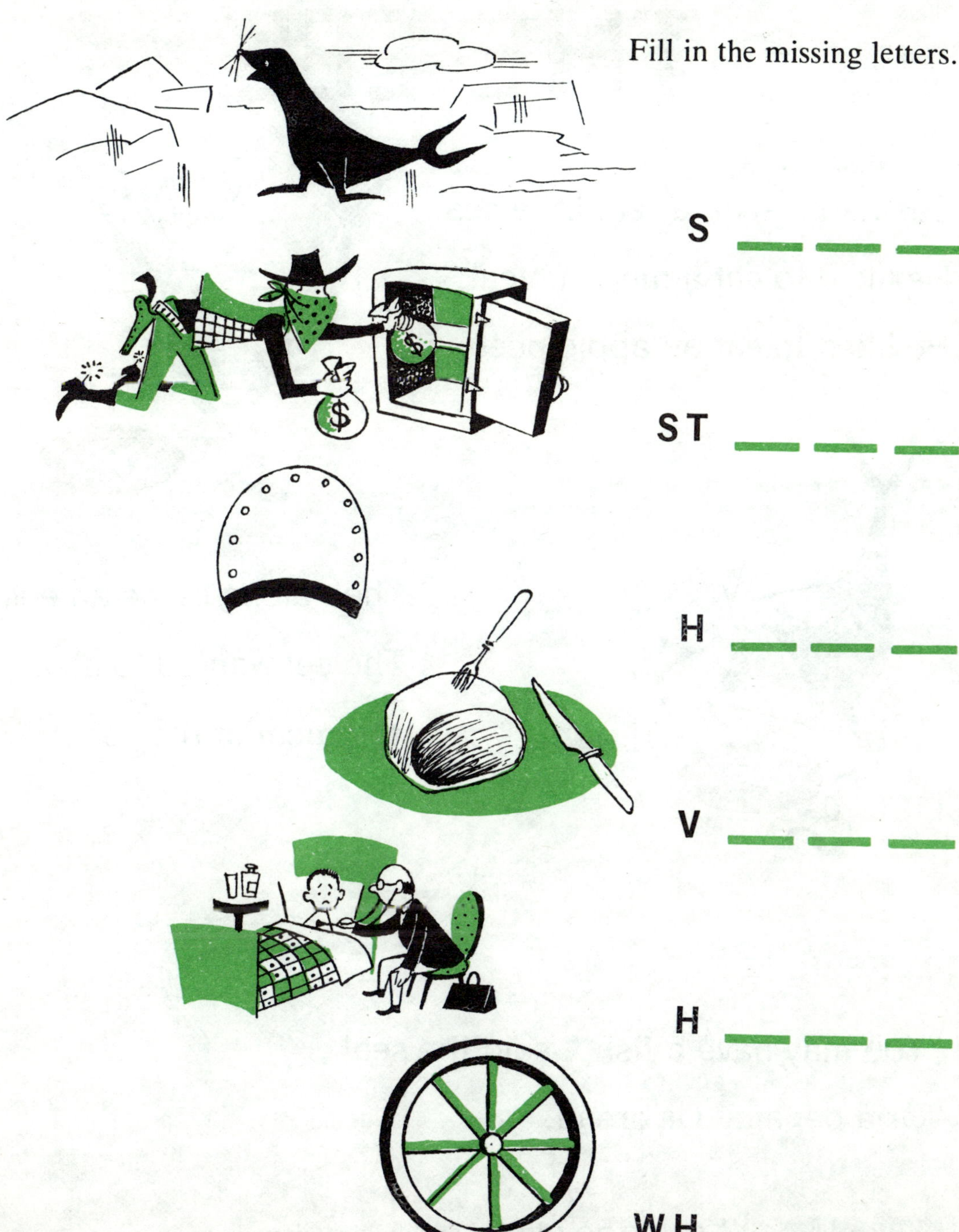

S ___ ___ ___

ST ___ ___ ___

H ___ ___ ___

V ___ ___ ___

H ___ ___ ___

WH ___ ___ ___

THE SEAL AND THE EEL

Sue had a seal, a real little seal.

He liked to eat a meal of veal.

He liked to eat an apple peel.

Then along came an eel.

The eel wanted to steal

the meal of the seal.

"You may have a fish," said the seal.

"Or a banana. Or bread."

"I want veal," said the eel.

"You may have milk," said the seal. "Or cake, instead."

"I want veal," said the eel.

"If you knew how I feel, you would give me my meal."

So the seal gave the eel his meal of veal.

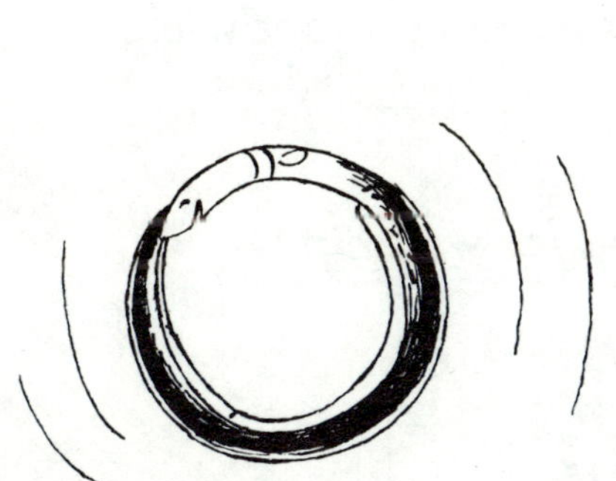

The eel, now well fed, put his heel to his head.

"See?" he said. "Now I am a wheel!"

CH

Here are some words which begin with the sound of CH.

CHILD	*A boy or girl.*
CHICKEN	*A tame bird which is good to eat.*
CHIEF	*The leader of an Indian tribe.*
CHEWING GUM	*It comes in sticks and you chew it.*
CHAIR	*What you sit on.*
CHEESE	*Swiss cheese is good in a sandwich.*
CHURCH	*A building used for worship.*
CHOP	*To cut with an ax.*
CHERRY	*A small red fruit.*

Fill in the missing letters.

CH ___ ___ ___

CH ___ ___ ___

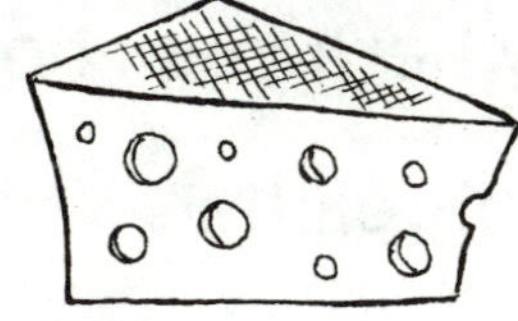

CH ___ ___ ___ ___

CH ___ ___ ___ ___ ___ gum

CH ___ ___ ___ ___

CH ___ ___ ___

CH ___ ___ ___ ___ ___

LOST CHILD

One day, in church, Sue met a little boy.

"How do you do," said Sue.

But the child did not speak.

"You must be lost," said Sue. "Tell me where your home is. I will take you home." The child did not tell her.

Sue took the child home with her. She gave him chicken and cheese and chewing gum.

The child had not had chewing gum before. He liked it fine, but he still did not speak.

Sue let him take her dog for a ride on a sled—the dog with the blue shoe and the red, red thread.

The child liked that fine, too.

Sue took him to the zoo.

There he saw a lion, and a bear

on a chair.

That was fine, too. What fun!

Then along came a man. The man was an Indian chief.

"Here I am, Father," said the child.

"So you can talk," said Sue.

"Why did you not talk before?

I told you I would take you home."

"Who wanted to go home?"

said the child.

B A

Here are some words which begin with the sound of BA.

BANJO *A musical instrument.*

BATH *You wash your entire body when you take a bath.*

BASKET *What you carry food in, at a picnic.*

BATTLE *A big fight.*

BATHROOM *The room where you take a bath.*

BATTLESHIP *A ship with guns.*

BANK *A place where people keep money.*

BAT *A small animal that flies. A bat looks like a mouse with wings.*

Fill in the missing letters.

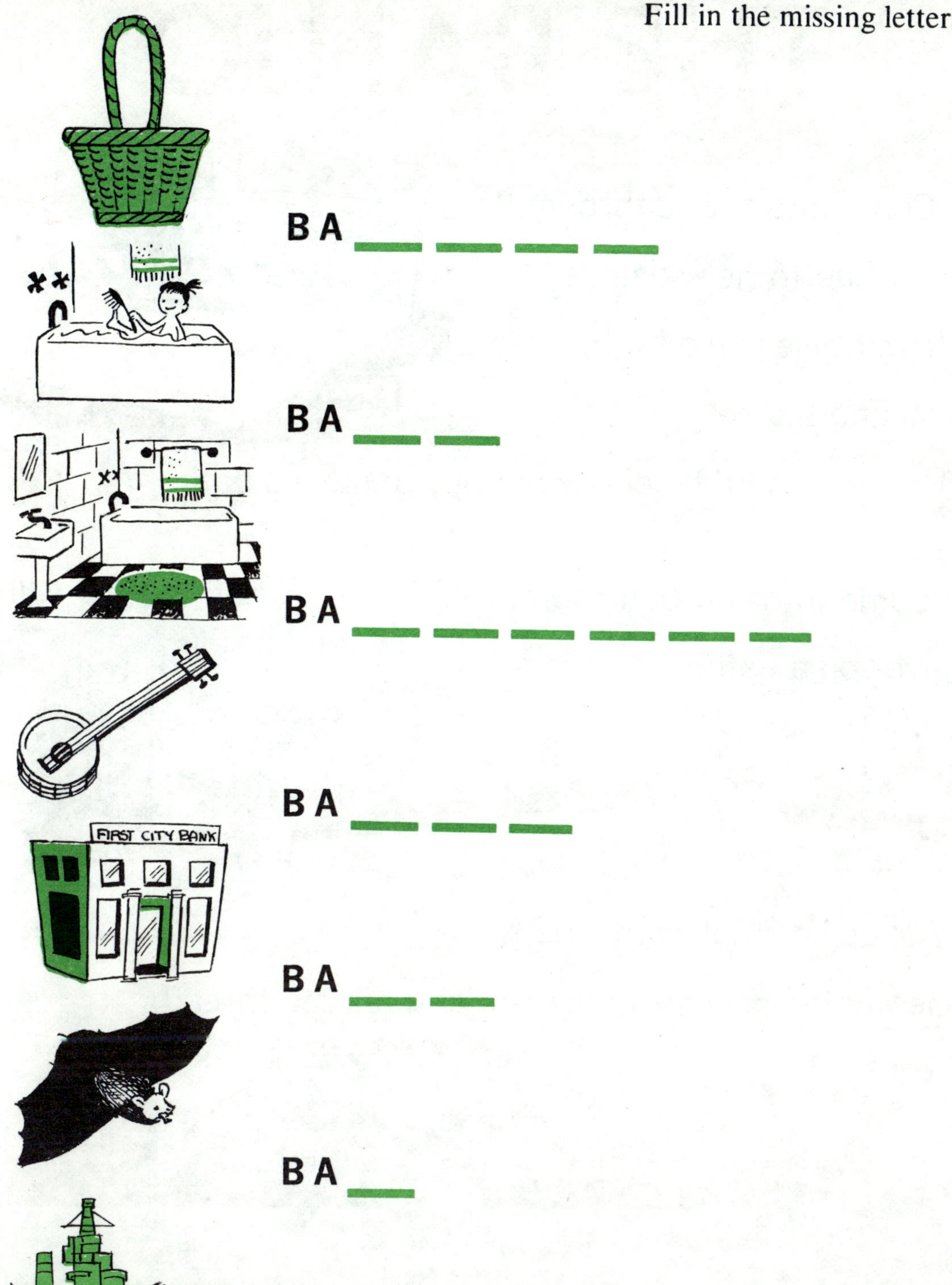

BA _ _ _ _

BA _ _

BA _ _ _ _ _ _

BA _ _ _

BA _ _

BA _

BA _ _ _ _ _ _ _ _

THE BANJO

"Come into the bathroom,"
said Sue to her seal.
"I will give you a bath,
you and the eel."

The seal and the eel were happy to have a bath.

"Come into the bathroom," said Sue to her dog. "I will give you a bath."

The dog did not want a bath.

He wanted only his blue shoe and his red thread.

Sue put the dog in a basket, and took him into the bathroom.

When he got his bath,
the dog gave Sue a battle.
Before he was through,
Sue had had a bath, too!

After that, Sue took her little bank
and went to the store.
There she got a banjo.

Sue gave the banjo to the child of the Indian chief.
My, he was happy.
He did not let the banjo out of his hand.

"Come into the bathroom," said Sue.
"I will give you a bath."

Do you know what the child did?
He took the banjo into the
bathroom.
Sue gave him a bath.
And he gave a bath to the banjo!

EE

Here are some words which end with EE.

TREE	*A large plant.*
BEE	*An insect which makes honey.*
KNEE	*You kneel on your knees.*
THREE	*The number after 2.*
FLEE	*To run away from something.*
FREE	*Not in a cage. A robin is free.*
SEE	*To look at something.*

Fill in the missing letters.

_ EE

_ _ EE

_ EE

_ _ EE

_ _ EE

_ _ _ EE

_ _ EE

EA

Here are some words which sound like the EE words, but are spelled FA.

TEA	*A drink.*
PEA	*A vegetable.*
FLEA	*A small, black bug which bites.*
SEA	*The ocean.*
PLEA	*A request.*

Fill in the missing letters.

__ EA

__ EA

__ EA

__ __ EA

__ __ EA

A LITTLE BEE

Sue went for a walk by the sea. She took her dog with her.

Now there was one thing that dog did not like. He could put up with a flea, but he could not stand a bee. You see, a bee made him flee. A bee was as bad as a bath.

Sue and the dog were at the sea, and along came a bee.

The dog ran and ran. He came to a tree. But so did the bee.

The dog ran and ran. He came to a house. He went in through the window. But so did the bee.

Sue came after them.

She had a talk with her dog.

"You are a big dog," she said.

"And it is just a little bee. Do not flee. Come home with me."

But the dog had to flee from the bee. He ran and ran. He ran on the sand. Then he ran into the sea.

One thing was good.

That dog did not have to take a bath that day.

AIL

Here are some words which end with AIL.

MAIL	*Letters.*
NAIL	*A piece of sharp-pointed metal used to hold wood together.*
SAIL	*The cloth on a boat which catches the wind.*
PAIL	*A bucket.*
SNAIL	*A small animal which carries its shell on its back.*
JAIL	*A building in which people are locked up.*
RAIL	*A track which trains roll on.*
TAIL	*The part of an animal which hangs down in back.*

Fill in the missing letters.

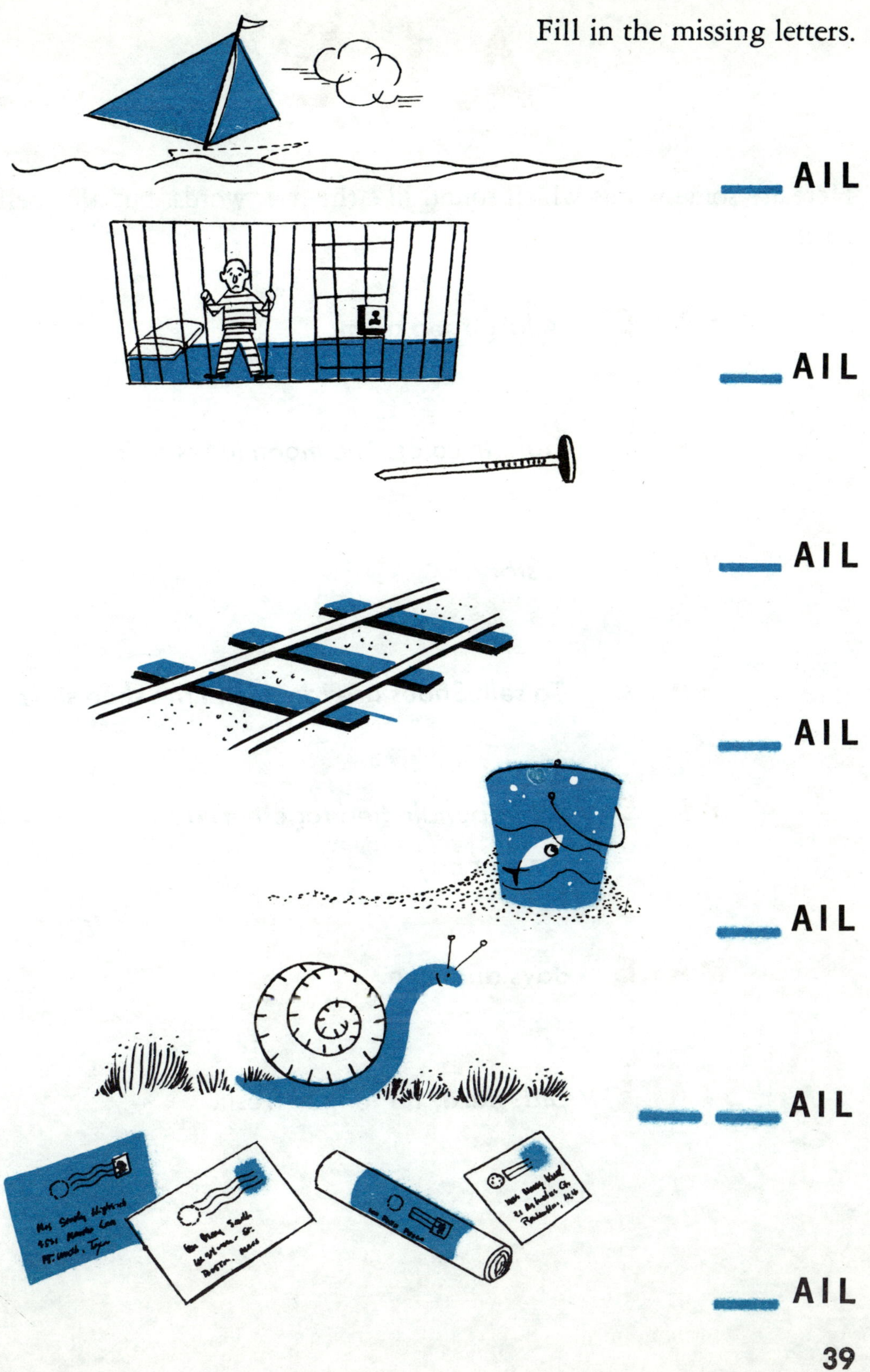

__ AIL

__ AIL

__ AIL

__ AIL

__ AIL

__ __ AIL

__ AIL

ALE

Here are some words which sound like the AIL words, but are spelled ALE.

WHALE *A large sea animal.*

PALE *Light in color. The moon looks pale.*

TALE *A story.*

SALE *To sell. Shoes are for sale in the shoe store.*

BALE *A big bundle tied together, as a bale of hay.*

MALE *Boys and men.*

STALE *Old; hard; no longer fresh.*

AIL or ALE

DO YOU KNOW WHICH?

WH ___ ___ ___

SN ___ ___ ___

S ___ ___ ___

R ___ ___ ___

N ___ ___ ___

J ___ ___ ___

B ___ ___ ___

HOUSE FOR ____

S ___ ___ ___

M ___ ___ ___

P ___ ___ ___

T ___ ___ ___

"MARY IS TAN. I AM ____."

P ___ ___ ___

M ___ ___ ___

THE WHALE

"Do you want to hear a tale about the sea?" said Sue to her seal and her eel.

This was the tale she told them.

One day, I went for a sail. In the sea, I saw a pale, male whale. What do you think he did? The pale, male whale went after a snail—a snail as little as a nail.

I took the little snail into my boat.

I gave him a pail to hide in.

I told the pale, male whale to go away.

But the pale, male whale did not go away. He wanted the snail in the pail.

"You may not have the snail," I told the whale.

"It is now my pet. I will take it home with me. You go away."

But the pale, male whale did not go away.

"If you do not go away," I told the whale, "I will put you in jail."

That pale, male whale went very pale. He did not want to go to jail. So away he went.

Then off we went, too,
the snail and I,
for a sail on the blue,
blue sea.

EAR

Here are some words which end with EAR.

DEAR	*A name for someone you love.*
SPEAR	*A long weapon with a point on one end.*
EAR	*What you hear with.*
YEAR	*From one birthday to the next is a year. A year is 365 days.*
HEAR	*When you listen with your ears, you hear.*
REAR	*In the back, or behind. Cars have front and rear seats.*
NEAR	*Close to.*
GEAR	*Part of a machine. Cars have gears.*

Fill in the missing letters.

__ EAR

__ EAR

__ __ EAR

__ EAR

__ EAR

EER

Here are some words which sound like the EAR words, but are spelled EER.

CHEER	*To make someone feel better.*
DEER	*An animal with horns.*
BEER	*A drink with bubbles on the top.*
QUEER	*Funny and strange.*
STEER	*To guide.*
JEER	*To make fun of.*

EAR or EER

DO YOU KNOW WHICH?

Fill in the missing letters.

D ___ ___ ___

G ___ ___ ___

B ___ ___ ___

CH ___ ___ ___

SP ___ ___ ___

THE DEER

One day, a deer came to the house.

Sue saw it at the window.

"Come in," said Sue to the deer.

In came the deer.

"Have a can of beer,"

said Sue to the deer.

The deer took the beer.

Do you think that is queer?

A deer who had beer?

"Now come for a ride in the car," said Sue to the deer.

The deer got in.

He sat in the rear.

A deer in the rear!

A deer who likes beer!

What a dear, queer deer!

Then the deer sat with Sue.

He wanted to steer! What a deer!

Sue said, "Now, dear, you may not steer. You sit in the rear, and be a good deer. Do you hear?"

To the rear, went the deer who likes beer. He was a dear, queer deer. And now he was a pet.

He met the seal and the eel.

He met the dog and the snail.

And he liked them all.

But he liked Sue more.

AR

Here are some words which end with AR.

STAR	*A star has five or more points. Many stars are in the sky.*
FAR	*Not near. The sun is far away.*
CAR	*An auto.*
JAR	*A big-mouthed bottle. Jars are to put food in.*
GUITAR	*A musical instrument with strings.*
MAR	*To injure; to spoil.*
SCAR	*A mark on the skin that shows where a cut or wound has been.*
BAR	*One of the rods that make a cage.*

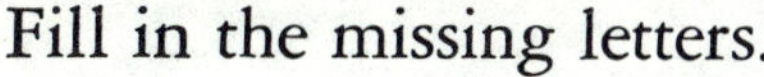

Fill in the missing letters.

THE SUN IS
--- AWAY.

___ AR

___ ___ AR

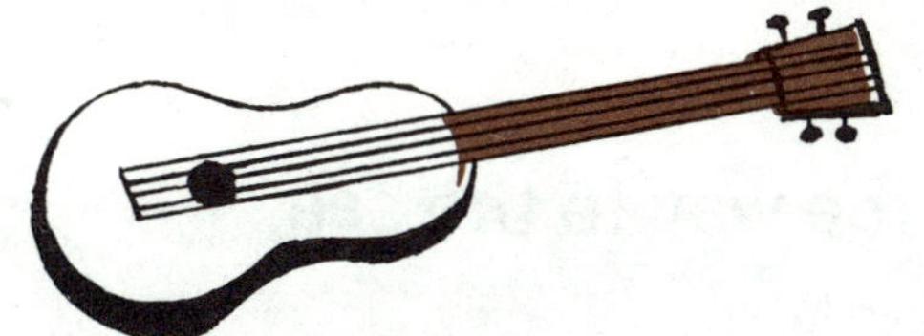

___ ___ ___ ___ AR

___ AR

___ AR

"A SCRATCH WOULD
--- THIS TABLE."

___ AR

THE STAR

The moon was up. Sue saw a star.

Sue went for a ride in the car.

She took her seal and her eel.

She took her dog and her deer.

She took her banjo and her guitar.

Away they all went in the car.

They went far. They went all the way to the sea.

Sue got out of the car.

And so did the seal and the eel.

And so did the dog and the deer.

Sue looked up.

And so did the seal and the eel.

And so did the dog and the deer.

Sue saw the star.

The seal and the eel saw the star.

The dog and the deer saw the star.

"What fun," said Sue, to the seal and the eel, to the dog and the deer. You came here with me in the car. And see? So did the star."

Then into the car went Sue.

And so did the seal and the eel.

And so did the dog and the deer.

They took a ride,

and when they got home

there was that star!

AP

Here are some words which end with AP.

TRAP	*A thing to catch mice and other animals.*
NAP	*A short sleep.*
MAP	*A picture of a country.*
CAP	*A small hat.*
TAP	*To touch lightly.*
LAP	*Your thighs when you sit down.*
WRAP	*To tie up.*
STRAP	*A belt-like fastening.*
SNAP	*To break quickly and suddenly.* *A piece of dry wood will snap easily.*

Fill in the missing letters.

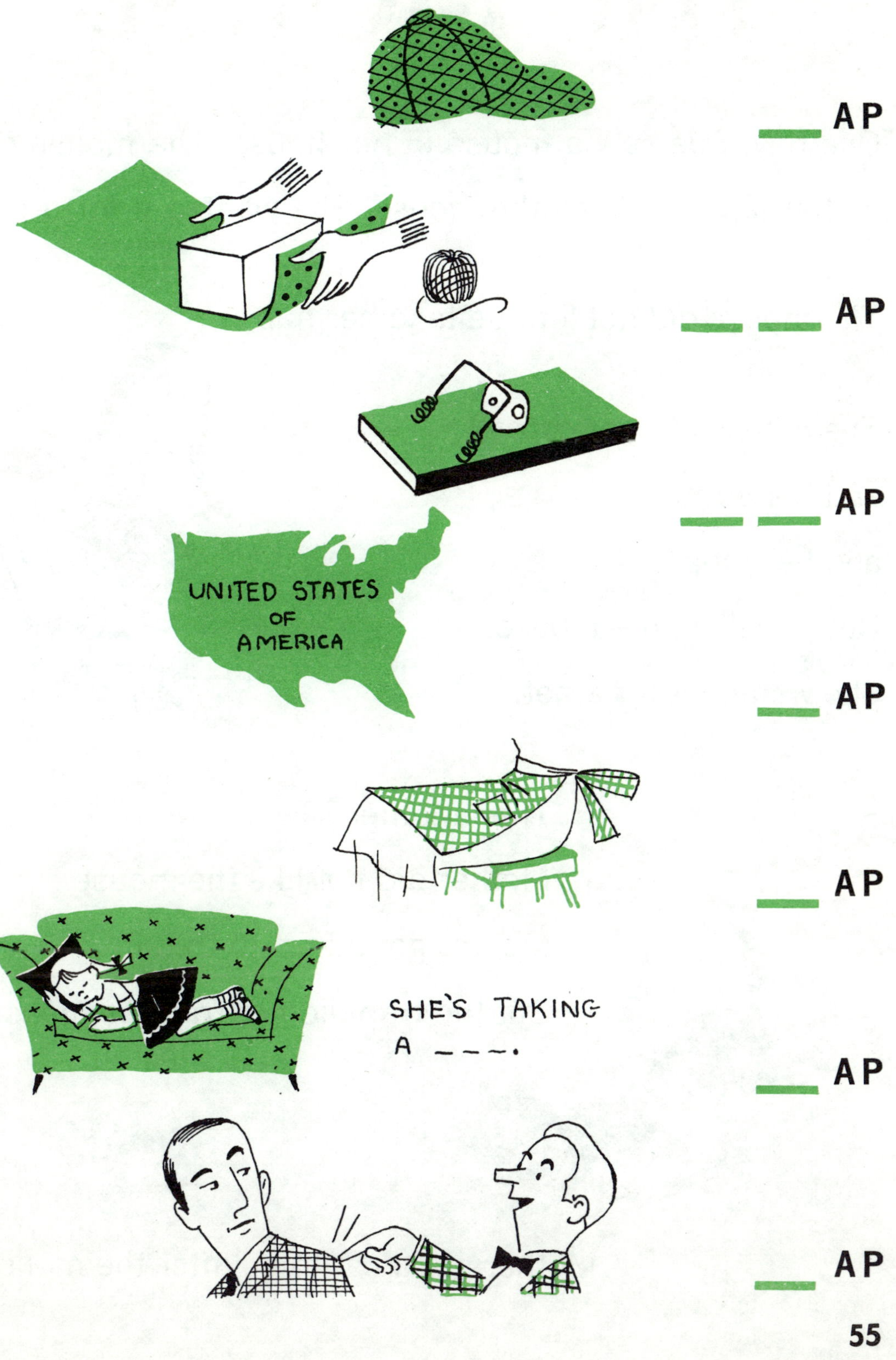

___ AP

___ ___ AP

___ ___ AP

___ AP

___ AP

___ AP

___ AP

THE MOUSE

One day, Sue saw a mouse in her house. The mouse sat on her lap. Sue liked the mouse. She wanted it for a pet.

The mouse did not let Sue take her nap.

The mouse ate her cap,
and her wrap,
and her map.
But Sue liked the mouse.
She wanted it for a pet.

Then Mother saw the mouse.
Mother did not like the mouse.
Mother got a trap to trap it.
But the trap did not trap the mouse.

Mother got a cat to go after the mouse.

But the dog went after the cat. So that was that.

Mother said, "Sue, dear. You have a seal and an eel. You have a dog and a deer. Must you have a mouse, too?"

"I would like to have the mouse," said Sue.

Mother said, "The mouse ate your cap and your wrap and your map. It went on your lap. It will not let you nap. Sue, dear, must you have a mouse?"

"I want very much to have the mouse," said Sue.

"What shall I do with you?" said Mother.
But she let Sue have the mouse for a pet.

AN

Here are some words which end with AN.

VAN *A large truck for moving furniture.*

BEGAN *Started.*

PAN *A shallow container for baking pies.*

FAN *A machine to cool air.*

RAN *To have already run. To run is to move as fast as you can.*

JAPAN *A country across the sea.*

CAN *A tin container of food.*

DAN *A boy's name.*

MAN *What a boy grows up to be.*

Fill in the missing letters.

___AN

___AN

___ ___ ___AN

___AN

___AN

ACE

Here are some words which end with ACE.

FACE	*The front of your head.*
RACE	*A running contest.*
LACE	*A pretty trim made of thread. Lace is used on dresses.*
SPACE	*What airplanes fly in.*
ACE	*A card with only one spot on it.*
PLACE	*A location; a spot. A bank is a safe place to keep money.*
TRACE	*To copy a picture by drawing over it on a thin sheet of paper.*

Fill in the missing letters.

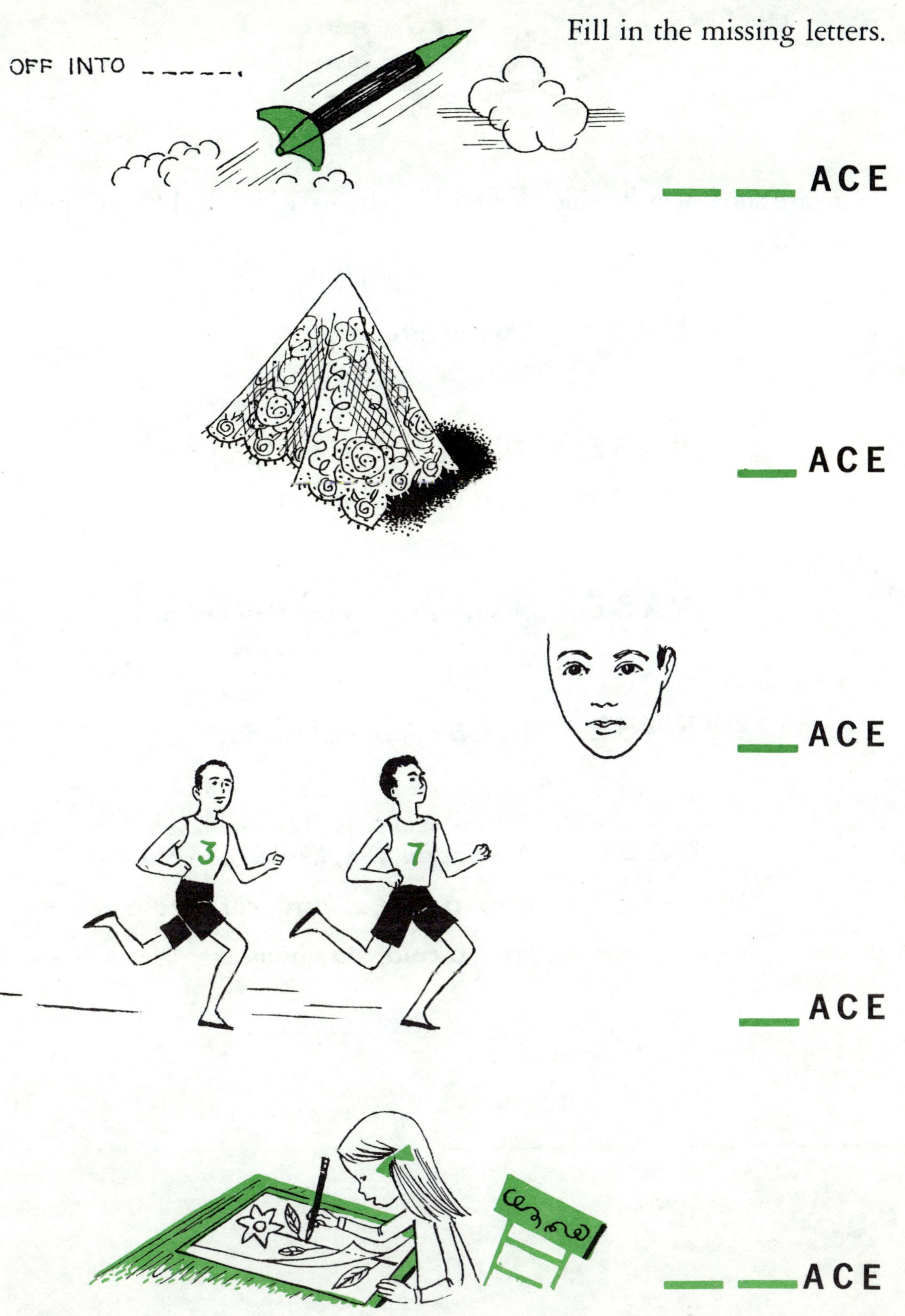

__ __ ACE

__ ACE

__ ACE

__ ACE

__ __ ACE

ASE

Here are some words which sound like the ACE words, but are spelled with ASE.

CHASE *To run after.*

BASE *The places baseball players start from and run to.*

VASE *A container to put flowers in.*

ERASE *To rub out pencil marks.*

CASE *A wooden box, like a case of beer. Also, a special instance: In case you have a cold, stay home.*

ACE or ASE

DO YOU KNOW WHICH?

Fill in the missing letters.

ER ___ ___ ___

C ___ ___ ___

V ___ ___ ___

F ___ ___ ___

B ___ ___ ___

L ___ ___ ___

THE LOST EEL

Sue sat down. She put her hand to her face. Her eel was lost.

Sue looked here and there.

Sue looked near and far.

But she did not find her eel.

Dan looked, too. He looked in this place and that place. He looked near and far. But he did not find the eel.

Then the seal looked for the eel.

He looked in a case of beer.

He looked in a little vase.

But he did not find the eel.

"I can find the eel before you can," said the dog to the deer.

"I can find the eel before you can," said the deer to the dog.

So they had a race—to see who could find the eel.

They looked in this place and that place.

They looked near and far. But no eel did they find.

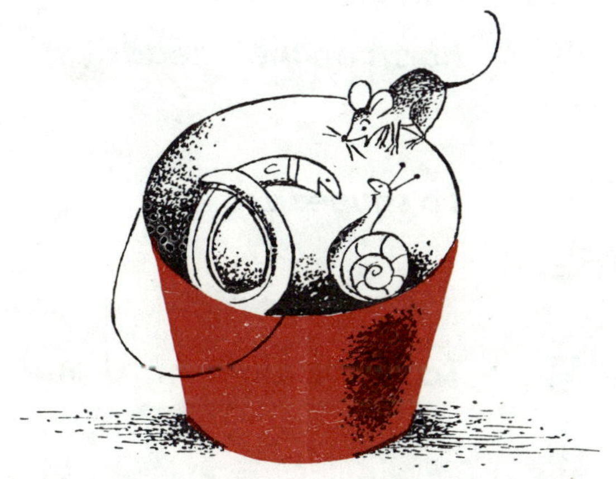

Then along came the mouse.

The mouse looked for the eel.

And there it was!

Where? In the pail with the snail!

Here are some words which have the letters AM.

JAM *A sweet, sticky spread for bread and rolls.*

CLAM *A small animal which lives in its shell. Clams are good to eat.*

HAM *The meat of a pig. Ham is good to eat.*

RAM *A father sheep. Rams have big horns on their heads.*

CRAM *To squeeze in.*

SLAM *To shut a door hard and noisily.*

Fill in the missing letters.

___ AM

___ AM

___ AM

___ ___ AM

___ ___ AM

Here are some words which contain the letters OW.

CROW	*A black bird with a loud, harsh voice.*
GROW	*To become bigger. You grow bigger every year.*
THROW	*To cast away, as to throw a ball*
SNOW	*White flakes that fall like rain.*
SLOW	*Not fast. A turtle moves in a slow way.*
BLOW	*To puff air out of your mouth, as when you blow out birthday cake candles.*
LOW	*Not high.*
MOW	*To cut grass.*

Fill in the missing letters.

__ __ OW

__ __ OW

__ __ OW

__ __ __ OW

__ __ OW

__ __ OW

THE O SOUND

Here are some words which sound like the OW words, but are spelled differently.

OH	*What you say if something hurts you, or surprises you, or makes you happy.*
SEW	*To make or mend clothes with needle and thread.*
DOUGH	*What biscuits or bread are made of.*
HOE	*A tool to dig up the ground.*
TOE	*You have five toes on each foot.*
WOE	*Trouble.*
FOE	*An enemy.*

Fill in the missing letters.

___ OE

___ OE

___ EW

___ OE

___ OUGH

THE PET CROW

Dan had a pet crow.
He took it with him
when he went to see Sue.

"Do you know," said Dan, "This crow was as little as my little toe. But oh, did it grow! Now it is as big as my hoe."

"Is that so?" said Sue.

"Yes," said Dan. "And my crow can do anything."

"Can your crow sew?" said Sue.

"I do not think it can sew," said Dan.

"Can your crow make the dough for bread?" said Sue.

"I do not think it can make dough," said Dan.

"Can your crow throw a ball?" said Sue.

"I do not know if it can," said Dan.

"Let us see if it can," said Sue. She got her ball. She gave it to the crow. The crow looked at the ball. Could it throw it? Not at all!

"Is there anything your crow can do?" said Sue.

"Oh yes," said Dan.
"My crow can play in the snow.
It can ride in my train.
It can steal jam from a jar.
It can eat a clam.
It can eat a ham.
It can see a ram.
And if it cannot chew
it can do anything a crow should do."

"Very good!" said Sue. "I think so, too."

ARE

Here are some words which contain the letters ARE.

HARE	*An animal like a rabbit.*
SQUARE	*A shape with four equal sides.*
MARE	*A mother horse.*
CARE	*To have a liking for a person; to fill his needs.*
SHARE	*A part of something.*
BEWARE	*To guard against.*
FARE	*Payment for a ride.*
STARE	*To look at something very hard.*

Fill in the missing letters.

___ ___ ___ ARE

___ ARE

___ ARE

___ ___ ___ ARE

___ ARE

AIR

Here are some words which sound like the ARE words, but are spelled AIR.

HAIR *You comb the hair on your head.*

PAIR *Two things which go together, as a pair of shoes.*

STAIR *Steps on which we walk up or down.*

AIR *What we breathe.*

FAIR *Pretty.*

REPAIR *To fix.*

CHAIR *What you sit on.*

ARE or AIR

DO YOU KNOW WHICH?

Fill in the missing letters.

CH ___ ___ ___

H ___ ___ ___

H ___ ___ ___

P ___ ___ ___

SQU ___ ___ ___

M ___ ___ ___

THE MARE AND THE HARE

Sue got two more pets—a mare and a hare. Where the mare went, there went the hare. Oh, what a pair they were.

The mare sat on a stair.

On the stair, sat the hare.

The mare got a square of cake.

The hare got his share.

Then they came face to face with the dog.

"Beware," said the mare to the hare.

"Take care," said the hare to the mare.

Then they came face to face with the deer.

"What is he doing here?" said the mare to the hare.

"Did you ever hear of a deer in a house?"

"No," said the hare. "And there is a seal here, too. Did you ever hear of a seal in a house?"

"No," said the mare. "And just look there. Is that an eel—on an apple peel?"

"That it is," said the hare. "My, but this is a queer place. Do you know what I think?"

"What do you think?" said the mare.

"I think this is just the place for us. I think we will be happy here, with Sue."

"That is funny," said the mare. "That is just what I think, too."

ARD

Here are some words which have the letters ARD.

YARD	*The land around a house.*
HARD	*Not soft. A stone is hard. Hard also means not easy.*
CARD	*A small piece of stiff paper, as a birthday card.*
GARDEN	*A place where flowers grow.*
GUARD	*To protect. Also, a man who protects.*
LARD	*Cooking fat obtained from pork.*

Fill in the missing letters.

___ ARD

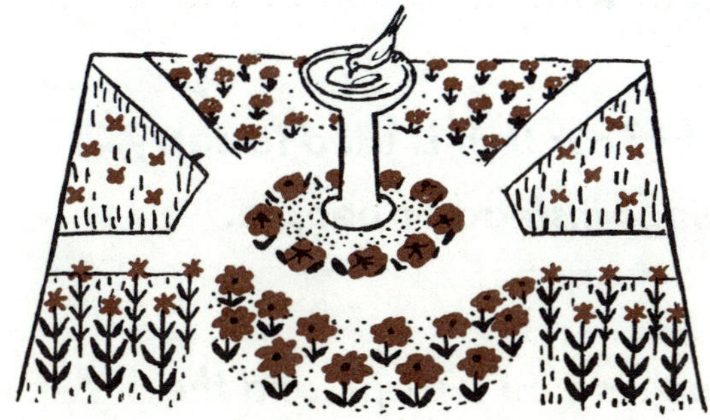

___ ARD ___ ___

___ ___ ARD

___ ARD

___ ARD

TR

Here are some words which begin with the sound of TR.

TRUCK	*A big car that is used to carry things instead of people.*
TRAIN	*You ride on a train, and the train rides on tracks.*
TRACK	*A track is a rail.*
TRUNK	*A big box to put clothes in. A trunk is also the lower part of a tree.*
TREE	*A big wooden plant.*
TRICK	*A stunt.*
TREAT	*Something special that you don't have every day.*
TRUE	*Not false.*

Fill in the missing letters.

TR ___ ___ ___

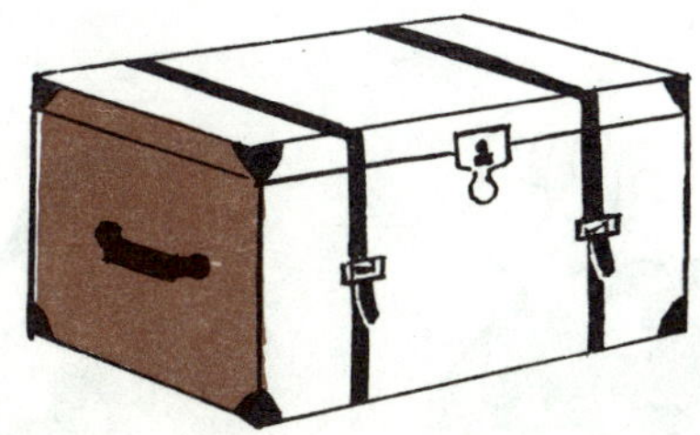

TR ___ ___ ___

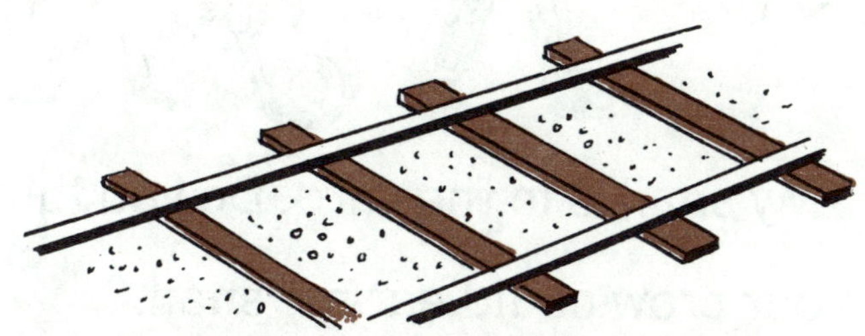

TR ___ ___ ___

TR ___ ___ ___

TR ___ ___

THE CROW

Sue took her snail out of the pail.

She put it in her garden.

Then Dan came to see Sue,

with his crow.

"Oh, dear," said Sue. "My snail is in the yard. Do you think your crow will find it? Your crow could eat my snail."

"My crow can do anything," said Dan. "But your snail is safe in the yard. He is too hard for my crow to eat."

"I know what I will do," said Sue.

Sue got her dog and her deer.

She had them stand near the snail.

She got her seal and her eel. She had them stand near the snail, too.

She got her mare and the hare. They stood there, too.

Sue had all her pets guard the snail.

Then, what do you know? Along came the crow. And he stood guard, too!

ING

Here are some words which end with the letters ING.

BRING	*To carry.*
CLING	*To hold on tight.*
KING	*The ruler of a country.*
RING	*You wear a ring on your finger.*
SING	*To make music with your voice.*
SPRING	*One of the four seasons of the year.*
STRING	*Cord.*
WING	*A bird flies with its wings.*

Fill in the missing letters.

FLOWERS BLOOM IN THE ______.

___ ___ ___ING

A BIRD HAS MORE THAN ONE ____.

___ING

THIS LADY IS TRYING TO ____.

___ING

___ING

___ING

JOAN LIKES TO ______ BEADS.

___ ___ ___ING

INK

Here are some words which end with the letters INK.

WINK	*You wink your eye when you play a joke on someone.*
BLINK	*You blink your eye when something gets in it.*
MINK	*An animal.*
PINK	*A pastel color. Baby girls have pink blankets.*
INK	*A writing liquid.*
THINK	*To give thought to.*
SHRINK	*To become smaller. Clothes sometimes shrink after washing.*
DRINK	*To swallow a liquid.*

Fill in the missing letters.

_ INK

"WILL THIS ------
AFTER WASHING?"

_ _ _ INK

_ _ INK

THE WIND MAKES MY
EYES -----."

_ _ INK

THIS BABY GIRL
HAS A ----
BLANKET.

_ INK

"I MUST ----- OF
THE RIGHT ANSWER."

_ _ INK

_ INK

INK AND ING

Here are some words which have both INK and ING.

shrinking *blinking*

winking *thinking*

Here are some words which have ING twice.

ringing *clinging*

winging *singing*

stringing *bringing*

Here are some words you know that have ING added to them.

wheeling *hearing*

bathing *stealing*

seeing *fleeing*

SPRING

It was spring. Dan came to see Sue.
Dan had his crow with him.

"Does your crow sing in the spring?" said Sue.
"My crow can do anything," said Dan. "Yes, he sings in the spring. Hear him? He is singing now."

"Oh," said Sue. "So that is what he is doing – singing. I did not know."

"What did you think he was doing?" said Dan.
But he gave Sue a wink.
He knew that his crow
did not sing well.

Sue looked at the crow.
And what do you know?
The crow gave Sue a wink.
He, too, knew that he did not sing very well.

ING or INK

DO YOU KNOW WHICH?

Fill in the missing letters.

W ___ ___ ___

S ___ ___ ___

W ___ ___ ___

DR ___ ___ ___

K ___ ___ ___

R ___ ___ ___

THE TRUCK

One day, Sue saw her mouse go up the trunk of a tree in the yard.

A truck was near the tree.
The mouse fell out of the tree.
It fell into the truck.

Before Sue could stop the truck, away it went.
She ran after the truck.
"Stop! Stop!" she said.
"You have my mouse!"

But the man in the truck did not hear her. On he went.

Then Sue saw Dan.

"My mouse fell into that truck!" she said.

Dan ran after the truck, too.

"Stop! Stop!" he said. "Give us that mouse!"

It was hard to race with a truck. It made Sue and Dan red in the face. But they just had to get the mouse. So on they ran.

The truck came to a train on a track.

"Look!" said Sue. "The mouse went into the train.

If we do not get him out, he will not find his way home."

"There, there," said Dan. "We will not let the train go off with your mouse."

Dan ran into the train.

"Here, mouse! Here, mouse!" he said.

"Here is some bread."

The train began to go.

Just then, out came the mouse.

And from that day to this, that mouse did not go up the trunk of a tree.

IGHT

Here are some words which contain the letters IGHT.

NIGHT	*When the sun goes down, day changes into night.*
RIGHT	*Correct.*
FIGHT	*A battle.*
MIGHT	*Maybe. Might also means strength.*
FRIGHT	*Fear.*
SIGHT	*The ability to see.*
DELIGHT	*Joy.*
LIGHT	*Not dark. The sun gives us light.*
TIGHT	*Not loose or roomy. Shoes that are too small for you are tight.*

Fill in the missing letters.

__ __IGHT

__IGHT

__IGHT

__IGHT

__ __ __IGHT

__IGHT

ITE

Here are some words which sound like the IGHT words, but are spelled ITE.

WHITE	*The color of snow.*
WRITE	*To make letters on paper.*
KITE	*A toy you fly in the sky.*
BITE	*To take a piece out of something with the teeth.*
POLITE	*To have good manners.*
RECITE	*To say a poem.*

Fill in the missing letters.

IGHT or ITE

DO YOU KNOW WHICH?

Write IGHT or ITE in the blanks.

WR___ ___ ___

SNOW IS _____.

WH___ ___ ___

"I PAINT WITH MY _____ HAND."

R___ ___ ___ ___

K___ ___ ___

F___ ___ ___ ___

POL___ ___ ___

RUNAWAY KITE

Sue and Dan had a kite. One day, the kite gave them a fright. The kite was in the air. Sue and Dan looked up at it. And oh! The mouse was on the kite!

"How did the mouse get there?" said Dan.

"I do not care how," said Sue. "Just pull the string—hard!"

Dan had the ball of string in his hand.

"All right," he said.

"But Sue, you could be more polite."

"Pull the string hard!" said Sue.

Her face was so pale it was white.

But the wind had the kite. The wind took the kite up and up.

The mouse was so far away it was hard to see it.

"Pull the string, quick!" said Sue.

"I will when I can," said Dan. "Sue, I know you love your mouse. But if you are not more polite, you and I may have a fight."

The wind took the kite
up and up into space.
Sue looked for her mouse.
But it was out of sight.

Dan did not have a fight with Sue. He had a fight with the wind, instead. He put all of his might into that fight. It was a very hard fight.

The sun went down. But not the kite.

"Will it take all night?" said Sue.

Just then, the wind let go of the kite. At last, Dan did pull the string hard. Down came the kite.

The mouse was still there.

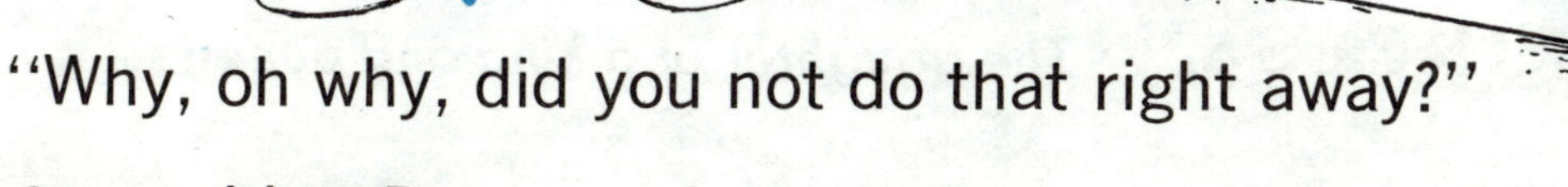

"Why, oh why, did you not do that right away?" Sue said to Dan.

"Sue," said Dan, "I could not pull the string hard until the wind let go. If I did, the string would break.

Now, do you see?"

"Oh!" said Sue. Her face was red.

After that, Sue was most polite.

ESS

Here are some words with the letters ESS.

DRESS	*Outer clothing worn by a girl.*
GUESS	*To suppose.*
MESS	*Untidy.*
LESS	*Not as much.*
BLESS	*To wish someone well.*
PRINCESS	*The daughter of a king and queen.*
UNLESS	*If not. I will not go unless you go.*
PRESS	*You press a flower in a book.*

Fill in the missing letters.

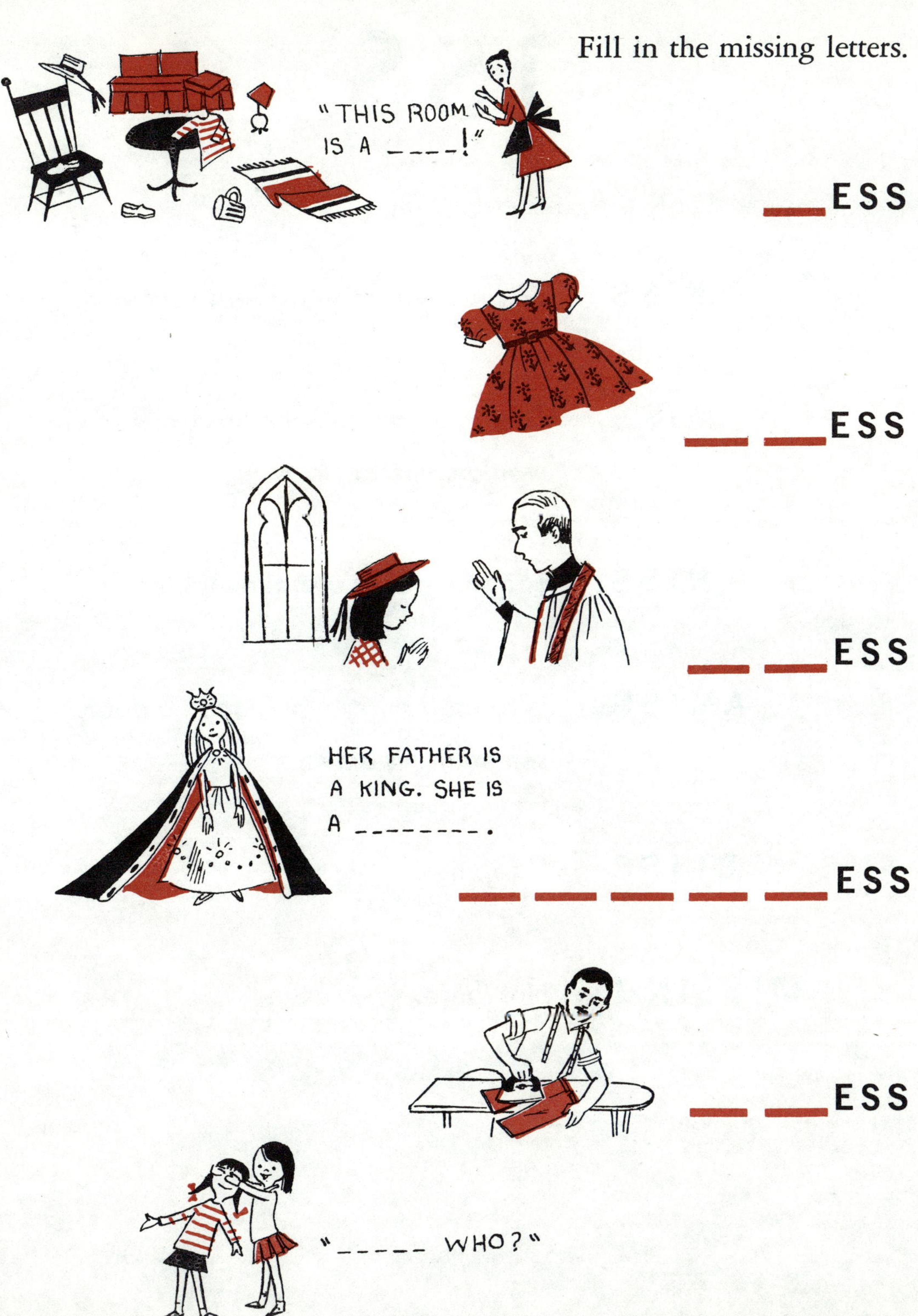

ISS

Here are some words with the letters ISS.

KISS	*To press your lips against someone.*
MISS	*To wish someone who has gone away would come back.*
HISS	*The sound that a snake makes.*
AMISS	*Wrong. If a key won't open a door, something is amiss.*
BLISS	*Happiness.*
MISSING	*Not there.*

Fill in the missing letters.

"WHAT HAPPINESS!
WHAT - - - - - !"

__ __ ISS

__ ISS

"ONE OF MY SHOES IS
- - - - - - - !"

__ ISSING

THE SOUND
HE MAKES IS
A - - - - .

__ ISS

"SOMETHING HAS GONE
WRONG! SOMETHING IS
- - - - - - !"

__ __ ISS

__ ISS

GUESS WHO

Sue went for a walk.

When she came home, she saw her dress on the floor.

The dress was a mess.

Sue could not guess who had made it a mess.

"Who did this?" said Sue.

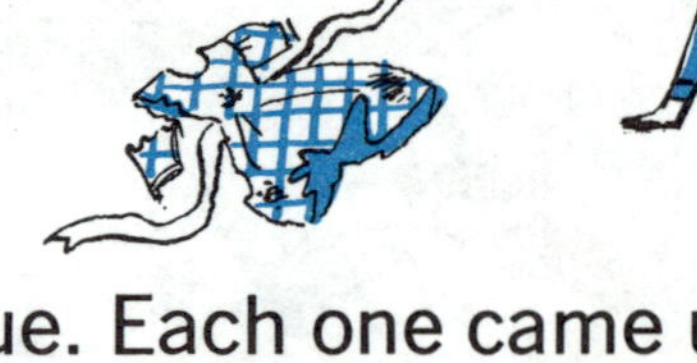

Her pets all saw that Sue was blue. Each one came up and gave her a kiss—the seal and the eel, the mare and the hare, the mouse and the deer.

But where was the dog?

The dog was missing.

Sue looked in the yard.

The dog was not there.

Sue looked in the bathroom. The dog was not there.

She looked on the big chair. The dog was not there.

Sue could not guess where the dog could be. She looked for him in this place and that. She looked near and far. At last, she looked in the right place.

Where did Sue find the dog? Under the bed.

"Oh, dog," said Sue. "You would not hide—not unless you were the one who made the mess.

Why did you do it?"

Sue began to think,

and then she knew.

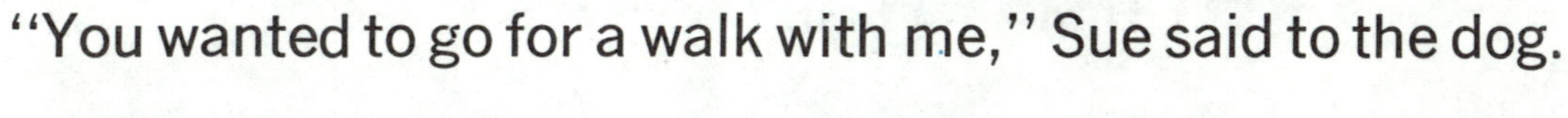

"You wanted to go for a walk with me," Sue said to the dog. "I did not take you. I was away all day. Did you miss me so much, dog? Did you miss me so much that you just had to be bad?"

The dog came out from under the bed.

He gave Sue a kiss.

He gave her his red thread

and his blue shoe.

And all was well.

Here are some words with the letters UM.

DRUM	*A musical instrument.*
GLUM	*Unhappy.*
GUM	*Something you chew.*
HUM	*To sing with your lips closed.*
PLUM	*A fruit.*
SUM	*An addition; a total.*
CHUM	*A friend.*

Fill in the missing letters.

UM SOUND

Here are some words which sound like the UM words, but are spelled differently.

THUMB	*The biggest finger on your hand.*
COME	*To move toward; to approach.*
CRUMB	*A tiny bit, as a crumb of bread.*
SOME	*A part of.*
BECOME	*To change into.*
DUMB	*Speechless; stupid.*
NUMB	*Without feeling. When your toes are very cold, they get numb.*

UM or UMB or OME

DO YOU KNOW WHICH?

Fill in the missing letters.

DR ___ ___

TH ___ ___ ___

PL ___ ___

CR ___ ___ ___

"PLEASE ---- TO MY PARTY."

C ___ ___ ___

G ___ ___

1 + 2 = 3

S ___ ___

THE CROW AND THE DRUM

Dan gave his crow a drum to play.

"This is the way you play the drum,"

Dan told the crow.

He went tap—tap—tap with his thumb.

But the crow did not play the drum.

Dan gave the crow a crumb.

But the crow still did not play

the drum.

Dan gave the crow a plum.

But not a tap did he hear on the drum.

Dan gave the crow an apple peel.

Still, no tap on the drum.

"Come here," said Dan to the crow.

"You just go tap—tap —tap. See?"

He went tap—tap—tap with his thumb.
"Now, you do it."
The crow gave Dan a kiss.
But he did not play the drum.
Then along came Sue. Sue had some gum.
"I will give some gum to the crow," she said to Dan.

"All right," said Dan. "But the crow did not want his crumb.

He did not want a plum.
He did not want an apple peel.
I gave him all of those things.
He still would not play the drum.
Maybe my crow is dumb!"

Sue gave the crow some gum.
What do you know?
What do you think?
The crow gave Sue a wink.
He took some gum

and he did hum as if to say, you are my chum.
Do you think that crow was dumb?

AME

Here are some words with the letters AME.

GAME	*When you play with cards, you play a card game.*
NAME	*People call you by your name.*
SAME	*Identical.*
BLAME	*To be at fault.*
SHAME	*To feel sorry.*
BECAME	*The puppy grew and became a dog.*
TAME	*Not wild.*
LAME	*To have a limp.*

Fill in the missing letters.

THIS POOR DOG IS
----.

___ AME

HER DOLL IS BROKEN!
WHAT A ______!

___ ___ AME

THESE TWINS LOOK
THE ----.

___ AME

"BASEBALL IS MY
FAVORITE ----."

___ AME

"I WONDER WHO IS
TO ----- FOR
BREAKING THIS."

___ ___ AME

"MY ----
IS JILL."

___ AME

THIS LION IS
NOT ----.

___ AME

IT

Here are some words with the letters IT.

FIT	*To be the right size.*
BIT	*A small amount.*
HIT	*To smack.*
SPLIT	*To divide.*
WIT	*Humor.*
OUTWIT	*To trick.*
OMIT	*To leave out.*
PIT	*The seed of a fruit.*
SIT	*To seat oneself, for example, to sit on a chair.*

Fill in the missing letters.

"WILL YOU -----
YOUR CANDY BAR
WITH ME?"

___ ___ ___ IT

"DON'T ----
MY REGARDS."

___ ___ IT

THE PUPPY --- A HOLE
IN THE CAP.

___ IT

"THEY DON'T ---."

___ IT

JOAN WILL --- THE BALL.

___ IT

"WE MUST ------
THE VILLAIN!"

___ ___ ___ ___ IT

A CHERRY HAS A ---.

___ IT

"HE'S CLEVER!
HE HAS ---!"

___ IT

ON WHEELS

One day, Dan came to see Sue. He came to see her pets, too.

He came on a thing he said was a train. To Sue, it looked like a big can. It had a fan on it, to make it go. It had wheels. And it had a pan to sit in.

"Come for a ride in my train," said Dan.

"Where would you like to go?"

"I would like to go to Japan," said Sue. "Would you?"

"I do not think so," said Dan. My train will not ride on water. You have to have a boat to get to Japan."

"Then I would like to go to a star," said Sue.

"The train will not go that far," said Dan.

"Then I would like to go and see the sand and the sea," said Sue. "That is just one block away."

"There we can go," said Dan.

Sue got on the thing that Dan said was a train. And off they went to see the sand and the sea.

They made a stop at the store for milk and cake. This they ate on the sand at the sea.

Then home they went, on the thing Dan said was a train. To Sue it still looked like a can with a fan. But she did not say so to Dan.

OUND

Here are some words with the letters OUND.

GROUND	*The earth.*
ROUND	*The shape of an orange.*
SOUND	*A noise.*
FOUND	*To discover.*
AROUND	*Near.*
BOUND	*To be tied to.*
POUND	*To hit hard.*
HOUND	*A kind of large dog, most often a hunting dog.*
WOUND	*Did wind, like a clock or a watch.*

Fill in the missing letters.

___OUND

"THE SHAPE OF THIS BALL IS ----"

___OUND

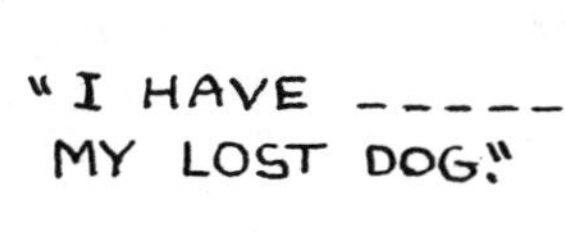

___OUND

"HE IS -----
TO THE TREE."

___OUND

"I HEAR THE
------ OF THE SEA."

___OUND

"I LOST MY PENNY
------ HERE."

___ ___OUND

THE GAME

One day, the dog made up a game that Sue did not like a bit.

He began to put things on the stair that should not be there.

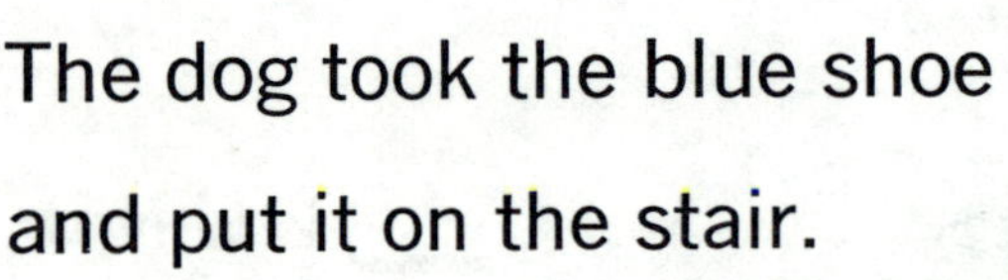

The dog took the blue shoe

and put it on the stair.

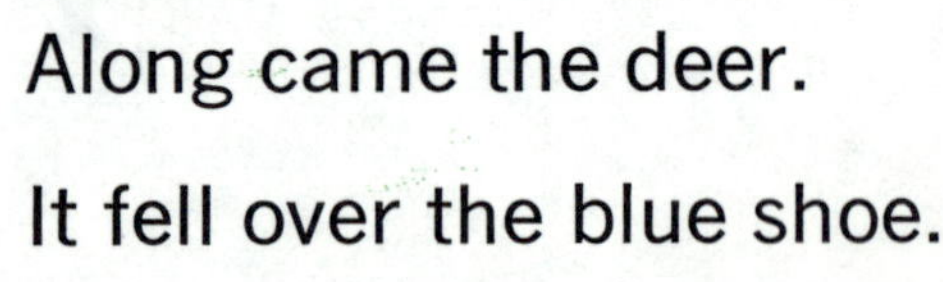

Along came the deer.

It fell over the blue shoe.

"Do you think that is funny?" said Sue to the dog.

"Shame on you."

She put the blue shoe away.

When Sue was not there,

the dog put the red thread on the stair.

The deer fell over the red thread.

"Bad dog!" said Sue. "You are to blame.

Have you no shame?"

The dog hid under the bed.

But when Sue went away,
he got the ball
and put it on the stair.
The deer fell over the ball.

"Now, you stop this game," said Sue. "Why, the deer is more tame than you. He does what I say, and you do not."
The dog hid in the bathroom.
But when Sue went away,
he put a book on the stair.

The deer fell over the book.
"Dog, dog!" said Sue. "What shall I do with you. If you do not stop this game, the deer will be lame." Sue hit the dog with the book.

But all the same, the dog put a bottle on the stair.

It did no good to hit the dog.

So this time, Sue gave him a bath.

The dog did not like the bath.
But all the same,
when Sue was not there,
he put a drum on the stair.
"For shame! For shame!" said Sue.
But the dog went on
with the game.

Then one day, a ball was on the stair. The dog did not put it there. He did not see it. He fell over the ball.

The dog did not think that was a bit funny.

At last, at last,
he gave up the game.

Sue was happy. She had wanted to outwit the dog. But she was not the one who put the ball there. It was the deer.

But now—oh no!—the deer began to play the game!

MORE PETS!

One day, Sue found that one of her pets was missing.

It was the mouse.
But where was he?

Sue and Dan looked for the mouse in the house.

All of the pets looked for the mouse in the house.

At last, the dog found the mouse.

The mouse was in the blue shoe.

And in the shoe with her were one, two, three, four, five baby mice!

Now Sue had all her pets. And Sue had five pets more. She did not know what her mother would say. But Sue was a very happy girl that day.

Doubleday Activity Books

Age 2 to 4

My Very First Storybook

Age 4 to 7

A Child's First Playbook
Fun With Dots—Rhymes for Tots
Keep Busy Book for Tots
A Treasury of Bedtime Stories

Age 5 to 9

Follow the Dots
Follow-the-Dots Stories
It's Fun to Learn
Learning Numbers Is Fun
Learning to Read Is Fun
Learning to Read Stories for Beginners
100 Learning Games
Riddles, Rhymes and Stories
Teach Me Numbers
Teach Me to Read

Age 7 to 11

Animal Fun Time
Crosswords Around the U.S.A.
Easy Way to Better Handwriting
Good Time Book
Holiday Funtime
Hooray for Play!
Keep Busy Book for Girls
Learning to Draw
Lots-To-Do Book
Step by Step Drawing
U.S.A. Fun and Play
Western Funbook

Age 9 to 14

Barrel of Fun
Baseball Funbook
Beginner's Crossword Book
Crackerjack Crosswords
Fun and Play all the Way
Introduction to Crossword Puzzles
Pencil Pastimes

Age 10 to 15

Fun Parade
Planets and Space Travel
Science Experiments
Simple Tricks